HENRY VIII
and the
INVASION
of FRANCE

HENRY VIII
and the
INVASION
of FRANCE

Charles Cruickshank

ST. MARTIN'S PRESS · New York

First published in the United States of America 1991
All rights reserved. For information write:
Scholarly & Reference Books Division,
St. Martin's Press, 175 Fifth Avenue,
New York, NY10010

ISBN 0-312-05196-4

Library of Congress Cataloging-in-Publication Data

Cruickshank, Charles Greig.
    Henry VIII and the invasion of France/Charles Cruickshank.
        p.   cm.
    Includes bibliographical references and index.
    ISBN 0-312-05196-4
    1. Henry VIII, King of England, 1491–1547. 2. Great Britain—
History—Henry VIII, 1509–1547. 3. Great Britain—History,
Military—Tudors, 1485–1603. 4. France—History—Louis XII,
1498–1515. 5. Anglo-French War, 1512–1513. I. Title.
DA337.C73 1991
942.05′2–dc20
                                                                90–46991
                                                                    CIP

Typeset in 11/12 Ehrhardt.
Printed in Great Britain

CONTENTS

LIST OF ILLUSTRATIONS

Photographs and illustrations were supplied by, or are reproduced by kind permission of the following: Windsor Castle, Royal Library, HM the Queen (6); The National Portrait Gallery, London (1, 12, 45); the Mansell Collection (5, 17, 46); Courtauld Institute of Art (11); The Bodleian Library, Oxford (3, 4, 9, 10, 23, 33, 34, 35, 36, 39, 40, 43, 48, 49); Society of Antiquaries of London (15, 16, 20, endpapers); Syndics of Cambridge University Library (2); Board of Trustees of the Royal Armouries (13, 14, 18, 19, 21, 22, 24, 25, 26, 27, 31, 32, 38, 41, 42, 44). Pictures 7, 8, 28, 29, 30 and 47 are reproduced by gracious permission of HM the Queen.

PREFACE

The plan followed has been to enfold in a narrative account of the 1513 campaign in France, which culminated in the capture and occupation of Tournai, the administrative, organizational, operational, and supply topics which seem worthy of separate treatment, without, it is hoped, seriously interrupting the flow of the narrative.

I should like to record my gratitude for help in various forms from Professor S.T. Bindoff, of Queen Mary College, London; Dr C.S.L. Davies, of Wadham College, Oxford; Dr Jeremy Goring, of Goldsmiths' College, London; Mr William Reid, of the Tower of London Armouries; and Dr Gabriel Wymans, Conservateur des Archives de l'État at Tournai.

C.G.C.

NOTE

The superior numbers in the text refer to the Sources which can be found at the end of the book.

The bracketed numbers in the text refer to the Notes which can be found at the end of chapters.

1 Objective

It was inevitable that Henry VIII should lead an 'army royal' into Europe within a few years of his accession, partly because he was by nature a bully, and partly to prove to himself, to his people, and above all to his peers the heads of state beyond the English Channel, that mastery of the art of war ranked high among his many accomplishments. Otherwise, he was but half a man.

The demonstration might be costly in terms of the wealth, effort, and lives of his subjects, but that was a secondary consideration. It would cost the king himself nothing. He would share none of the discomforts of the rank and file, and virtually none of their dangers. He would not suffer when 'grey-bearded winter began to show his face' and caused the 'decrepit shivering soldiers to complain and groan to each other'.[1] When he moved from one place to another he would not drag himself and his equipment on foot over muddy tracks, but would make the journey on horseback in the heart of a 'plump' of his most trusted guards, who would count it an honour to die in his defence. It was, however, unlikely that any would enjoy this privilege, since troops of light cavalry would scour the countryside to send back information about the movements of the enemy so that the king might be kept at a safe distance, 'for great honour consisteth in the safe-keeping' of the king and his Council.[2] Moreover, when there *was* the possibility of contact with the enemy, his royal person, unlike that of the yeoman archer or billman, would be protected by an ornamental steel casing weighing between sixty and seventy pounds. His table would be no less heavily laden than at Greenwich, nor his servants less numerous. Wherever the campaign took him he would sleep comfortably in his own bed, not necessarily alone, in a portable wooden house, the component parts of which needed twelve carts to carry them; or if he preferred it, in a palatial marquee hardly less magnificent than one of his bedchambers at home, and certainly not under a hedge or in a hut improvised from branches.

He would encounter few real hazards. Some tactical blunder by the higher command might suddenly engulf him and his bodyguard in a major battle from which there was no escape save through hand-to-hand fighting. He might be unlucky enough to find himself without armour in the path of a bullet fired at random from the walls of a besieged town, as did Sir Edmund Carew.(1) This indeed was a possibility envisaged by the Bishop of Durham when he drafted some notes about the plan of the 1513 campaign. He suggested that the king should not himself take part in any siege but remain with his retinue at a safe distance. In the bishop's view there were good reasons for this precaution: 'in the conserving of his noble person dependeth the weal and surety of his realm and all the nobles and others of his army, whereas of the contrary (which God

Henry VIII c. 1520

defend!) the loss and destruction of all may follow.'[3] The odds against this sort of mishap were very long, however. Indeed, bearing in mind the fate of Sir Francis Brian, who lost an eye in the jousts,[4] or of Henry II of France, who lost his life, it might be argued that the monarch was in greater danger in a tournament than on the battlefield, especially if he forgot to close his visor, as Henry VIII himself once did, leaving his face 'clean naked' and an inviting target for his adversary's spear.[5]

Nevertheless, the young king's burning desire to play a leading part in the affairs of Europe, fanned by the lingering influences of the code of chivalry, demanded conflict with more edge to it than jousting in the tiltyard. Existing rivalries happily provided him with an argument for moving from sham to real warfare. In November 1511 England joined the Holy League, an alliance with the papacy, Venice and Spain (and later the Empire) aimed at keeping France from dominating Europe; and in doing so she became involved in a war in which she had far less to gain than any of the other contestants.

Henry's father-in-law, Ferdinand of Aragon, had his eye on Navarre, a French possession straddling the Pyrenees; and if Henry wanted to offer himself as a cat's paw for furthering the aims of Aragon, Ferdinand certainly had no objection. Maximilian, the Holy Roman Emperor elect, who controlled the whole of what is now Germany, Austria, the Low Countries (through his grandson Charles), and a large part of north-eastern France, and was also

The coronation of Henry VIII and Catherine of Aragon

nominally responsible for some adjacent territories, saw in Louis XII's ambitions a threat to the security of his own dominions. He too was delighted to accept England as an ally, although he did not believe that her help would have much effect on the balance of power in Europe. In Italy Pope Julius II was the victim of French aggression, and also welcomed any support that Henry could provide.

There was, of course, no real need for England to become thus entangled. Henry had inherited peace with France under a treaty made by his father in 1502, which was renewed (as it had to be on the death of the sovereign if it were not to lapse automatically) on his accession in 1509. It would have sufficed for the moment if he had concentrated on developing his father's careful and unspectacular domestic policies, leaving the warring monarchs of Europe to sap each other's strength. It was too much, however, to expect the virile Henry, just into his twenties, to stand idly by, content to control the modest destinies of England from the Council chamber, when the spirits of St George and the illustrious fifth Henry held out the promise of honour and glory on the battle-fields of Europe; and if he had to pick a quarrel, France clearly selected herself as the most appropriate enemy. Her traditional links with the boorish Scots, who were always a potential menace to England's northern marches, her perpetual threat to the English town of Calais and to English shipping in the Channel, and her hostility to the papacy, which England still supported, all singled her out.

Henry made his first tentative interventions in the military affairs of Europe in 1511, when, in spite of the opposition of some members of his Council, he sent a force of about 1,500 archers under Thomas, Lord Darcy, to join Ferdinand in a campaign against the Moors of Barbary; and a force of the same size under Sir Edward Poynings, Warden of the Cinque Ports and former Lord Deputy of Ireland, to support Margaret of Savoy, Maximilian's daughter, against the Duke of Guelders. The latter expedition did quite well, in spite of having to operate in difficult territory, for the leader was a man of great experience and ability; but the former turned out to be a wild-goose chase.

As soon as it reached Cadiz in the south of Spain, Darcy was told by Ferdinand that he had decided to call off his campaign against the Moors and to keep his forces at home to defend the country against the French. The English commander was furious at this change of plan, but there was nothing he could do about it, except curtly to refuse Ferdinand's invitation to come to Seville to receive his thanks at a banquet, and head for home. It was just as well that his troops were not put to the test, as they found the heat of the Spanish summer too much for them. Hall records that they 'fell to drinking of hot wines and were scarce masters of themselves. Some ran to the stews, some brake hedges, and spoiled orchards and vineyards and oranges before they were ripe and did many other outrageous deeds.'[6]

In spite of this débâcle Henry sent a force in the following year under Thomas Grey, Marquis of Dorset, to join Ferdinand's troops in an invasion of Guienne. Grey had come near to execution as a traitor in the previous reign, but his jousting skill had restored him to favour in the eyes of Henry VIII. This expedition also accomplished nothing, partly because of the incompetence of the leader, partly because lack of pay and victuals induced the troops to mutiny, but